Minding the Spectrum's Business

— Irene Mitchell —

FUTURECYCLE PRESS

www.futurecycle.org

Library of Congress Control Number: 2015939849

Published by FutureCycle Press
Lexington, Kentucky, USA

ISBN 978-1-938853-81-4

For my husband, Mark—the page turner within.

Contents

— III —
Full Planetary Swoop

Acknowledgments

— I —
Upper Level Disturbances

...such disruption may spark unexpected clouds and precipitation....

Charting the Expanse

A spare room, though it be sparse,
is the handout I crave,
an extra room which cannot be shared—
for the one within
is given it as a favor
and place to rest
from discomfort or cold.

Do not mind living
in the extra room,
for it is only a spare bone
and a respite.

Looking through binoculars
at the hawk in a tree,
one can see the day is all about finding
a spare meal which, when digested,
enables a thing to better fly.
Restlessness is the only price to pay,

paving the way for the rest of the saga
and the eye that goes with it.

The flinty couch is mine alone
and so is the shivering white lunarscape
out the window.

An Eye at the Keyhole

His eye at the key-hole, this is what the poet sees...
an unending spiral....

—Cocteau, **Blood of a Poet**

Scent of perfume
when there is none,
just the atomizer.
Windows open to a breeze
what little there is
as the pendulum swings.

There should not be pepper in the little mill,
but there is some.
This is the portrayal through the keyhole
of a poet's room.
It wants to be painted
after the rubble is cleared,
leaving titanium-white walls
and a small—let's say meditation bench—
for authenticity.

A daily peek through the keyhole
is music for the mind,
an unending spiral
which lends composure to battle,
at least while the grass is still greening,
which is for only a moment in time,
a cunning move
to claim space, every inch of ground
covered
except where deer have trod in the night.

All Rise

It is worth descending
if only to rise.
That is what they tell me
when I rise
from a bed of water, a waterbed so buoyant
it is great to be on land again.

Worth the weight
when I rise
as a balloon released
from the breakfast nook
having buttered and jammed
and worked the grapefruit segments
counterclockwise.

A luminous break
from the fast held overnight
with no great suffering,
breaking from a sleep
wherein I floated without assistance
under a baby blue, arched ceiling
of sapphire boats.

Smartly garbed, first in thought I rise,
then in deed
and prepare to enter the workplace.

There, they all rise
to greet me
for I have been gone so long.

Very Rich Hours

Now to drop with a thud silver linings
and settle for the familiar.

A whistle is heard from high
in a poplar;
a satisfied, yes, a smug
little mockingbird calls,
and had I not wandered out at noon
in the field beyond this solitary acre,
I'd have listened to its raptures.

I'd have supervised
as the four-footeds run for cover where I roam
to hyperventilate deep in their holes.
(What are you renegades up to?)

Yes, skunks and coons
do visit this spindly acre at night.
I have been able to notice
a few fast-moving rumps
fleeing by moonlight.
But when my little world
in Spring is greening,
they do not dare appear
because I bare my teeth
and wave some stinging nettle.

I mind this property without a telescope.
Each task, well done,
can be set aside in all tranquility.

Self-scrutiny remains a fever.

Surveillance

Note three dandelions
craving recognition in a late autumn field,
how they spy on the goldenrod,
how they emulate the breeze.

What I said to my audience
then made up of three dandelions
and sun flashing through clouds,
was only to enliven their game
played out in that secret
outdoor anatomy club we all know about,
in which I had no high stakes
having a field of my own to return to,
a field laid out for winter rest.

What I say to my audience
now made up of ice melt and morass
is that to mind and measure a field
is a lonely amusement.
The stakes are high. Need to see those acres
burgeoning.
Need to feed those treasured cows.
I place my bets, inspect and keep a watch.
This is how it is.

A man cannot change his stars.
How is it with you?

Pachelbel Farm

Ondine, Palisade, Quasar
and others
(who's counting?)
come running
all of a color
cows of brawn and sheen
and sublime largess

come running
when is heard
the scoop into the grain
dipping,
the grain into the trough
spilling

whereupon, all of a copper brown
they come running
Bountiful, Charlemagne, Monsoon
and others
and that, in cow terms,
is what it means to be alive.

Complacencies to Live By

Western thought proposes
that the spirit
journey toward its given end
but make it a splendid, the best ever
end, one with a surplus of surprises
as when the boardwalk scale
for fifty cents announces
Your weight and your destiny.

The best destiny ever:
intimacy with light
and shadow,
each step of the way recorded
with an ear
for the discordant,
an eye for the disconcerting.

And toward journey's end
who would not miss the sky most,
its scarlet twists and pink brocades,
an embroidered sky
to keep the self in earthly thrall
even through thunder.

Pink and Blue

For Tess and Joe

Only if there is enough celestial blue
will the snow below appear pink.
That is the view from inside the room,
an undistracted observation
which, as reality, holds together.

More precisely, to see this phenomenon
the eyes must be closed, the room sunlit.
Then open
to receive the vision.

A tidy compendium of recent visions:

freeloading swallows
hitching an azure ride
on the harried hawk's back;

blue heron, granite throne,
subjects snail and sea,
thrown spray at every boulder.

So a happy heart
leaves the imagined shore.

But only close eyes in a sunlit room
to receive a gilded glimpse
of Tess and Joe
kite-flying on the pink hillside.

Flesh, cloth, air.

Momentum

As leaves dress a tree,
so do I fix and fuss,
so do I trim.

As bark encircles ring,
so do I envy protection,
so do I limit and exclude.

Sun torques
to my lodge
at the crux of noon.

Letter E catches beams
while the rest of the weathervane
poses, does not turn
though the heron is hot to fly toward W
and all along Cape Flattery.

Constructing reveries of this sort
is helpful to the heart, though most illusions
gather momentum
on their own,
just windforce, sheer bravado,
hum of voices,
submission,
jangling of the mind's keys
between stations.

Appointment in Sumatra

A tree grows
in the vestibule,
tall and green
as vexation.

The doctor is late.
This might as well be Sumatra,
home of the disappearing rhino,
where heat is high
and ire combustible.

Do not ask questions, only answer.
Strip to the waist, coward,
or flee to the Ring of Fire
where all is livelier than here.

When we talk about blue moons,
we mean
hardly ever, that is—never
will I leave the earth
(no matter what she says)
without a merry goodbye.

Invincible

Or so I dreamed (I was).

Reminded of the hardships that ensue
when one tries to eclipse the actual,
and so blinded by the white page (was I),
it became my duty to fill it.

I understood that the onus was (on me) to also
rectify the damage done,
any fallout
from the previously overwrought page,
since I had planned for its content
to be transcendental,
a Zen tranquility to it.

This scrutiny of my pages (by me)
is for my own good,
so longing for quality and correctness (am I).

But desire, like the bird that mocks,
empties, fills (repeat) in all its aspects.

Existentialism 101

Definition of a soul? Anyone?
And where found?
Somewhere deeply buried.

A clean white placard, a cloth,
most likely cotton, most likely
starched.

The ear calls the soul,
calls the starched cotton
to arms.
Something is up.

Something the opposite
of a placid mooring.

Anyone? Offer a dollop
of pudding,
a real taste of the concept
that is soul,
which concept arrives around age three,
the age at which one learns
to keep a lid on any moral or spiritual
underpinnings
while keeping pristine
the starched white cotton pinafore.

About Beauty

About Beauty and its revelations
(which Memory is keen to keep
as if a bird ushered in
actually fluttered),

we are poised to rediscover
a flock of willets rising from the mangroves,
daffy clouds high above,
a promise of south wind;

poised to remember
that onyx has a place on the palette,
that incoming waves are made of it.

Our dwelling's downward from Hull Bay
where garden and sea suffice as World.

We are the couple on the littoral far off.
(He takes her picture.
She fluffs her skirt.)

Softly Through the Woods

On the forest floor,
a Pandora's box of leeks and quirky ramps
yielding
as moss to a footfall.

Softly through the woods
footfalls scatter swallows and pipits
(their cries of lamentation)
from woodland chasms.

This is how Memory operates—
a drift
of feathers, a thought taking wing
as it did when original—
the first thought about Love,
the now fabulist memories
upon which to build a bed of grass and nettles.

Deep Attachment

Evening is nigh,
horizon sedate.
It's time we began to bicker.

Your raptor's beak looks ready
as a sharpened point to penetrate.

Tonight we will argue love, lust,
and jurisprudence.

You suggest rules of order,
but I am a fountain
of extraneous perplexities
and melancholy redundancies.

I preen and posture, you uphold.
How I adore the precious exchange of minutes,
taut and slowly pulsing.

We play out to the end, a civil court.
There is no reliquary
of bent knives, spent forks.
With my permission you advance
to kiss the wounded breath of love
before going in for the kill.

Manners at the Round Table

That is why
there was so little known then
about courtesy, that rarity,
though not as rare as chivalry,
that relic
of the age of Sherwood Forest's band
of sweetheart thieves.

That is, if by thieves
one means grabbers of goods
or affections.
That is, if by recipients of the bounty
one means those to whom the grabbed goods
are presented.

I steal for you because it's empowering.
I cook plucked goose for you
                        because I love you,
and on the hit list
is the helmeted guinea fowl.

Hold the sweetbreads! Buff the armor!

Flimsy vows to protect and tend
are made in a frenzied state
in which emotions eddy, a pond
ducks have dipped into,
and what we wouldn't give for a little down.

Three-Season Conversation

As a refrain to the banging door
silk-screened for summer,
you have promised
to uphold some measure of silence
as required for hydration, balance,
and survival
because noise intrudes and taunts
create pure burn.

If not silence, then sweet-talk
through winter's healing plaster—
waterfall in celluloid rapture,
ground a permafrost
upon which we walk prudently.
There are snowgeese in the far field,
hundreds of white notes
like invitations.

Then in springtime comes your appeal,
impertinent lover revving across the dunes
in your metallic blue with the top down
to entice me.

The roof rides up
when wind whips hard
and rain gravitates to the windshield.

Precious Metal

Laburnum: All parts of the tree are poisonous: roots, bark, wood, leaves, flower-buds, petals, and seedpods.

There are witnesses;
ebony trunk of poisonous Laburnum
takes equally poisonous Golden Blossom
in lethal matrimony.

Perfumed racemes like golden chain
droop wantonly over night's unlatched fence,
plotting to forfeit servitude
for seduction.

A fine way to mix up a world
is to announce a tree's true nature.
In the face of deciduous beauty,
who would not be quick to sample?

It is reported that every mistress becomes
a poisonous golden chain.
She wants to know the truth
of every minute,
take a private look into every second,
mine every nanosecond for repetition
or impending news.

She wants to find an easy way
through the softened crust
after a rain.

Striking a Chord Across Time

In the beginning, love was a plainsong
heard simply as wind
rushing through hectares of tall grass.

As only love can witness,
the grass yielding
engendered the next chord.

That chord investigated
the crucial—
how love deepens.

There was also a time when rain
was fresh rain
for flower and basin.

One cannot ask *why*
about love or a term of apprenticeship,
only retrieve and remember.

— II —
Gamma-Ray Glow

*...dark matter is exposed but its composition
remains a mystery....*

Animals

Let us say of the wolf packs
they are too like wolves
to regret the aftermath,
their trail like berry's blood—
their announcement.

Let us say of the shooter
he is too diabolical
to question his intent,
his trail like berry's blood—
his dénouement.

To ream through flesh,
rip out the maw—
is allowed and approved
only by tooth or by claw.

If feathers fly
and cries lift up
that moment before eternity,
then berry's blood—
our view from here
looks smart
looks mean
as *natural* should.

But if shooter is beast,
his is a crime
bloated and gaping,
a bloody engagement
which savages peace
at a kill rate
of twenty to one.
Then done.

Loose Change on Capitol Hill

Please empty pockets of money, phone, keys,
intelligence.

The slightest hesitation
in the vestibule of the hall of mirrors
announces that one has entered.
It is wise to keep going.

One does not want to meet
the wrong people here.

When next the invited enter
the White House Blue Room
for the inauguration,
the mirrors are all too reflective.

The Press Secretary has enumerated upon this point
ad infinitum to an *ad hoc* group
of the fair and the fey.

One could say the next sparking minute
of life should not be wasted on follies
such as the kind which occur
upon looking into a full-length mirror.
Who is the master then, one wonders,
or mistress.

Running for Office: Queen of the Realm

I do not know from what rich artery or vein
these slogans flow,
but they are savvy slogans, in all their majesty
fine enough to repeat.

That is what my constituents tell me,
and they clamor for more choice bits
as the evening unfolds.
So I deliver
as if I were serving up a pretty tabbouleh
laid out with some naan.

It is almost a profession.

After the campaign we convened
at the Hotel Clinton, seventy steps
upward from the heart of winter
to where the sun splayed its dusty shafts
back down to the courtyard. The builders
had provided an exit to the roof
and there we meandered,
a sidelong drift of a climb
necessitating, at the top, an equilibrium adjustment.
I had taken a seat on a canvas chair and was sweetly
backed up to a pillow,
when Conscience, breathless, arrived.

Dream Gazette

A bomb dropped in our valley.
Silence, silence.

This is a fiction
but someone is looking and feeling—
someone walking by the railway bridge.

Everything looked satisfactory.
Sun was about right,
hard white and shadowless.

Despite fission and fusion,
most of the oysters in nearby estuaries
remained intact.

Someone rescued from the compost
thirteen long-stemmed pink-tinged roses
newly thrown upon the heap.
If that someone were from Brazil, he could earn
one *brasileiro*
for every rose
and at two *brasileiros* per dollar
this would mean his emancipation.
In this fabrication, though, the bomb did not drop
in his *favela*
but in our valley.

Dreams like these come more frequently now:
someone is either walking away
with someone or getting an invitation
to bed.
A telephone inside me rings.

Evolution

Do you like this garden, which is yours?
See to it that your children do not destroy it!
—*Lowry,* Under the Volcano

Ear relays the pain,
inner ear clamoring
for an altered state
in which sound
becomes enchanted,
leaving only melody, whisperings, rush
of wind and water.

Ears, what's wrong?
Stampedes, avalanches, felled
trees, screaming prey
in the mouths of coyotes,
the avenging gunshot, not
that sweet whiz of the arrow.

The space lab
sent a probing camera
into a world
older and fatter by one hundred million years
than was originally thought,
a world which, in its vast carelessness,
harbored theories of evolution dense as magma—

when we had thought it to be
an enchanted place filled with melody,
whisperings,
rush of planetary wind and trickling water.

The Tribe that Hid from Man

And so today, nothing is in jeopardy.
Alleluia, at least, for that.

I grant myself permission to take repose
upon a bench which maintains its brilliance;
fountain just as white
and a bird sipping there.

I don't want to go beyond
these first hundred yards,
which will prove
no one dear has yet parted company
and peace persists.

That the Kreen-Akrore, forced to broach modern times,
forfeited to prospectors, cattle-breeders
and enemies
their peaceful existence and original
primal territory
only served to secure their demise and degradation.

Paul McCartney performed his version
of *Kreen-Akrore* on iTunes—
nothing but drumbeats and birdcalls
of the Brazilian rainforest,
also available as a cellphone ringtone.

Myself, I have always liked the rim:
a glass, a pond, a moon,
Safe there from din and clatter,
minding only the spectrum's business.

Life as an Enchanted State

*The world of the living contains enough marvels and mysteries
as it is...it would almost justify the conception of life as an
enchanted state.*
                            —*Conrad,* The Shadow-Line

And in that happy consciousness
is found all the marvels of this world.

Suppose it to be a world
without symbol or dread;
that is enchantment enough
for me.

Presume it is a world of composure
and beautiful speech.

Speculate upon this world
as if humankind were steeped in a blissful
poultice, pain stopping suddenly
over a wounded countryside.

Let me be honest while the blue hydrangea
still is blue;
into this dream I melt.

It is the dream of Blithewood Garden
where phoebe sings *phoebe,* cardinal sings *figaro,*
ah, what frenzy!
and lark flaunts his *ave maria.*

Tempus Athol Fugard

It goes back to what I think is man's central dilemma:
the fact that life dies.... And the passing of those seconds...
it's death knocking at the door.

—Fugard

The hours are served up
a savory essence,
two dozen bites
on each white plate,
each morsel adding to Afrikaner history.

Fugard would take an interest
in any world of secrets,
ever one more morsel digestible,
a playwright's longing to clear the plate
before praxis.

There's a deuce of a lot of blue
in South Africa,
to say nothing of the red ambiance
after a massacre.
Fugard with blue iris
(that's the chancy part)
stands guard at the door

whilst time, a precious trickle of ivory,
scars the ravine.

Contemplating Death in Venice

Tadziu smiled at him...the smile of Narcissus...flirtatious,
curious and somewhat tormented, infatuating and infatuated.
—*Mann,* **Death in Venice**

It wasn't merely the strawberry,
but the nourishment;

not only the pair of spectacles,
but the vision;

not just the wearing of these,
but the surveillance
of Beauty;

classic beauty cast in marble,
or shattering beauty
(vibrato for cello and strings)
of the Polish youth, Tadziu,
"u-u-u" at the end,

desired by Aschenbach (stream of ashes),
cremation of the world's ugliness,
the fire before the gong,

flames ignited by thought, not deed:

You must never smile like that
at anyone....

Aschenbach pursuing the grail
with such buoyant delicacy
as when a stream of ashes
has been poured into the sea

which ashes then are summoned toward eternity
astride a wave.

Light Lesson

The Upper Side of the Sky, 1944 oil on canvas
Kay Sage, Surrealist

The shadow of my house
falls on the lawn.
It looks like the shadow
of a barn
but it is the shadow of my house falling
on the lawn.
There never was a barn
and this can be proven by the shadow
of a chimney on the roof
of the house's shadow.

Furthermore,
the upper lode of sky
has spun a shadow
between the door and kitchen floor
but it's not my checkered floor,
it's not my kitchen from which a yellow curtain flutters—
though the idea of a yellow curtain fluttering
takes hold like a stark new city of implausibles
serving to minimize
the cozy shadow of my house.

It's clear that light (so loud when near,
ear stands in for eye)
obliterates obscurity
as light is meant to do)
and clear
(footfalls on the checkered floor,
the curtain waving near)
that though home is where the light is—
intimacy with shadow
makes one free to walk the world.

Protection

I enjoyed a place at her table
till things took a turn.
She said the culprit
was miscommunication
but I knew it to be her sense
of singularity—
that she considered herself an orchid,
petals shimmering
with the wind's tremolo.

Thus freed,
I began to love the hours,
felt destined to see the world
as an artist—
not just a curious traveler
seeking orchids at every clime.

There were intervals
during which flame gave way to desire
for company,
as when atop the waves
flash little peaks of sunlight, millions
per second.

A courier bearing torchlight
brought me news:

Be always in the company of metaphor.
Do not be without your protection.

Mapping the Home Territory

Looking for E. St. Vincent Millay

Before you can say Addis Ababa
or Haile Selassie, once fond Emperors
of that grassland biome, Ethiopia,
she had disappeared
into a thicket of moss and myrtle,
to which place I was to follow

in the morning vapors
to pick up her intermittent signals
and trace her wanderings
as I would with any precious map
of Africa
or the hills of Austerlitz, New York.

Before you can say Noho, Soho,
or Dumbo,
I picked up her scent, for she had trampled
wild oregano in the aforementioned hills.
When morning vapors vaporized
and cirrus overpowered cumulus,

I rode all afternoon, not very merry,
in hope of sighting her
on the Staten Island ferry.
A lead played out in Camden, Maine.
By then, I had assumed the identity
of a pickpocket navigating his plunder

On the third day I rested.

I will pause to mention the simple affection
I have for my work,
for the tension that comes as a right
with every mission.

Maps wear, umbrellas wither.
Yet, I lumber on,
resisting arrest,
explaining, pointing
to the red lines on the map's code,
the green boxes at the center of a sphere.

Am I near?

Classical Music for Your Monday

We're at the Press and Blend Café
next to Jarita's Florist
where the sun singes
this afternoon redder than Jarita's dahlias.

This is Woodstock,
a place where neighbors
can lean over the fence
and talk about encroachment.

Conversations stem from meetings
or retreatings to the chapel with its slight
scent of myrrh.

A new condominium tower is rising.
Do not break the peace, the parish prays,
by including a roof.
It will need to be hammered.

Bicycle bells ring between hammerings.

The tower materializes.
The few who get to dwell in an artist's studio workshop
have finally found a garden
with more clover than grass
and cannot now be seen from here.

Hurricane S

Were it not for the river overflowing
on a sunless day in October,
everyone would have been refreshed and cozy
after work
as is the mean for Autumn in New York.

I don't want to re-envision that day.
By concentrating
I can get a grip on fantasy.

In this fantasy,
a hurricane uses a password
for permission to come ashore.
May I?

I don't want to re-live that period
when havoc heaved its burden
upon the innocent.

We saw the stars flatten
the way they do in a tempest.
One could say about this claim
there's no tomorrow in it—

but morning, like an attendant peacock
that puffs up and thrills, invited everyone
to find a moment to turn,
knowing that the burning shaft of light
at the escape hatch down the runway
will quickly vanish
as salmon through a gauntlet of bears.

Swizzle Stick

Waves have lost their fizz,
all being as it should on a dull night
in Atlantic City after the storm
when gambling on anything
is of no use to the universe.

If one could siphon energy
from catastrophe,
harmony from ruin,
there would be left a rich little world
of dignity and sharp ideas.

As it stands now, the warning
is to stay safe because clusters of dignitaries
from the Venus Casino
are arriving
to foment their theories about winning
and replenishing,
but those theories are ignorant of strategy,
airy foam on a wave,
wind moaning through the arcade.

Eurhythmics

Eurhythmics: A system of dance used for therapeutic purposes.

The caller at the Swoon Dance Kitchen Bar
gave these prompts:

First, imitate a raindrop.
Punctuate the sod with heavy footfalls
and wedge a bit of moisture
between a man and his row of marigolds.

Next, mimic a snowflake.
Execute a delicate six-minute whorl
with intent to expire
in perfect fall
at some crystalline outpost.

Now quick-step
to a pulsing battlefield and depict how soldiers
deflect the pain to another spot
and die to a gun-salute of thunder.

Art cheats Death, they say.
A curious and festive notion.

Please change partners and dance to that.

Love Ever, Sam

Throughout the petty ambush
of bees among the daylilies,
I read the letters
of Samuel Beckett.

Sam to Tom McGreevy:
I like that crouching, brooding quality in Keats.

Dublin is lovely with no trains and buses,
the hills and sea seem to have crept nearer.

The letters state every indolence
and indiscretion,
excel at sympathy and empathy,
now and then take sides.

I read while waiting
on the green, awash with daylilies.
It is a prescient morning in May
where beyond the courthouse Corinthians
murmurs a small choir of maples.

A juror, enlisted for impartiality,
is taking his oath to tell the truth
while another with potential
reads *The Tempest.*

Ariel to Prospero:
Hell is empty, and all the devils are here.

Sam to Tom McGreevy:
I would like to live in a perpetual September—
watch kites fly.

Love, ever.

Holdings of Value

For Carolyn

Take Peace,
everyone's darling;
composure
after panic is derailed.

Take Light,
the luster of *forge ahead,*
the amber of *wait-here-a-moment.*

Take Music
as if unafraid.

Read love-letters
as a precious ore.
(So long on tap have they held a breath.)

Write your letters to the world, cherishing
the outspread lexicon.

— III —

Full Planetary Swoop

*...celestial objects orbit, each entity rounded
by its own gravity....*

Inquiry and Pursuit

There was chiming
all over town
and the high moorlands.

This "Carol of the Bells"
so near Christmas
I thought might slake my thirst
for a sweet procession of tidy hymns,
which hymns would then avert
such shiverings
in the cold places of my heart
and across the moorlands'
snow-laced heather.

Whether it was the chiming
or the tenor's rendition
of "There is No Rose of Such Virtue,"

a warming trend
prevailed
all over town
and the high moorlands,
as if prevailing winds
could entirely alter the escape route.

The wind has stirred
and is rising.

A Vague Unease

Apprehension!
That is why the clock
faces the wall
or no clock at all.
Side-splitting laughter
would be a relief, or at least
a tender burst of sunlight
at some hour in the day,
preferably toward late afternoon.
Then by evening, oh, yes,
a reprieve does come
with the layout for a simple supper,
a stick-to-the-bones confabulation.

Do not get me going—though a tangent
often serves to titillate
the original story line,
especially when delivery is replete with sighs
of either dissatisfaction
or satisfaction,
as when ginkgo's lobed leaves fall,
pretty scalloped fans
underfoot.

Oh, yes, this is a vague unease,
a mild complaint of unknown origin,
what is called idiopathic,
and I never know what small gripe
will get it going,
a bee, for example, on the screen
or a weakness in the floor.

Pes Anserine

That's what hurts.
The conjoined tendons of the pes anserine
splayed out as a goosefoot
and swelling at the inside knee.
Do not cry out until it worsens
at pre-dawn and our ordinary walk
to the river becomes a dumb notion.
We do not need to see
those rampant Canada geese
and their copies. Harpies all.

Across the river, percussing
like a complaining knee,
there are crashings at the coal plant, a sifting
and dumping of minerals, a grimy waste
in toxic plumes.

What befalls in the celestial commotion
of the pre-dawn universe
is more reminiscent of a hell filled
with repetitive signatures
like the knee's grum S.O.S.

Save Our Souls.
Be light and heavy.
Live and thrive.

Personal Advice

Above all, do not use caution
but go haphazardly, taking what is there
as if a baby bare among the ferns,
careless and conjecturing.

If you smell fire
when there is none,
maybe it's the sun descending
or the lamplight glaring down the road.

As long as there are luna moths
on the moon's surface
or red corn on the earth's,
be more or less inclined
toward speculation rather than convention.
May this advice,
without shock waves to the knee,
carry you home
to opposite poles of Heaven's sphere
where revolve the battering stars.

Self Portrait with Sour Grapes

Lyric hardball
is to be played with reverence
in the mind's court,
a game of solitaire
with sonic underpinnings.

The court is limed. I play
within its boxes
until I am the only one left wondering,
What is the point
of rules which kill momentum?

Better to play on a sunless day
as eyes have no tolerance for strobe.
Brow should remain cool throughout.

The grayer the day, the higher the stakes
because darker, as later,
implies a boundless field.

Cunning moves are made
in the misty relevance of twilight,
one's own overcast moody empire.

In this realm there is no need for triumph
or fleeting reward,
just a small honorarium
for forging the fiord
when light was loved
and it did not hurt to falter.

Objective Correlative

Why persist in gaining entry
when the gates have closed,
the objective shimmering still
in twilight.
Or when night comes, why sustain
the longing to search the halos of the moon
and high places.

Sun is ever thwarted
and garden's winter funk
destroys the last leaf's hold.

Summits are not so high
they can't be reached in a balloon,
lofty, like desire,
but attainable.

Once, in the balds of the Uwharries, a desire arose
to run across the grassland
with the horses—
but only rabbits came.
Somersaulting with them,
I was able to discern a view
of the objective, shimmering still
in twilight.

Attitude

This is in reference to the ache
that launched a thousand lies,
created furrows and arches
on this brow, this back.

I present to a panel of my peers
a case of misappropriation
of the truth
concerning certain well-rubbed drawings
on the wall of a cave,
especially that of a girl retrieving water
from a rivulet.

The truth is, I am she
and I was carrying the water in a pitcher
to my shelter a furlong away
and through the cornfield.

When the alphabet slipped from my lips,
I set down the pitcher and with full composure
wrote six chapters of a story.
Every line was hyperbole
but that furthered my advantage,
which was that no one represented on the cave wall
would listen, anyway,
to these delights and scraps,
and that is how I wanted it,
so tired was I of one-dimensional company.

In the following year, however, I had much of import
to share concerning actual events
but calling two-dimensional company to attention
proved impossible so that the ache
escalated to aggravation,
creating furrows and arches
on this brow, this back.

Progress

Temporary as lamplight in early morning,
last night's longing
etherizes to a mist.

The particular becomes the common.
This is a useful construct,
similar to perfecting one's first language
before learning another.

To formulate new parameters by noon
requires stealth and strategy
but nothing comes.
A plan is needed
so one is chosen
from those in transit.

It is the plan to staunch the heart
by encapsulating in one furtive move
all sun motes in the watch area
and storing them in a pocket pouch
to dispense as needed.

There is nothing so satisfying as a resolution.

A Clean Slate

The plain white wall:
no disturbance,
no tears, no dallying.

Flushed from alluvial clay
and washed.

Seeded at the frost line
and sprung.

A bare white wall
suggests such beginnings.
We shall press for more.

First, tie up your sleeve.
Then, buckle your shoe.

There will be no comeuppance
when A outshines B.

We do not grieve betterment.
Just keep the vernacular clean.

A Right Mind

The strategy I love most
is to accept every cube and curve
aimed this way
no matter how harsh or calamitous,
with the proviso
that the trajectory
be honest as the hour is long.

This is how to amass a museum collection
of modern predicaments.

Amendments to this formula
are considered whenever the arrow
does not hit home.
Why give in to an apotheosis
of fervent supposition
when one can say, I learned
so much today
from the Curator!

Sun and Water

There are enough spies in the land
to find, finagle, and deliver
the object of desire—
information,
just information.
May delivery come as neatly
as a thrice-folded napkin
under a fork
just to the left of the white plate.

What will I do with so many bits
of information?
Gather and store in the root cellar
until cohesive.
Scrutinize the profusion for any unwanteds.
Seems so easy.

There may come a time, however,
when all I need for sustenance
will be sun and water.

To the Heart's Architect

I sometimes dream of a larger...house...of only one room, a vast,
rude, substantial, primitive hall, without ceiling or plastering....
—*Thoreau,* Walden

Let shell become home
without lathe or eaves
so light source may reach each way round.

Avoid mishap through measurement.

Construct below frost line.
Eye angles.
Mark distance between egg and sun.
Plan to face the early red noons that knock.
Capture water fast-flowing from a stream
of icy fissures.

To lie undisturbed, as clam in clay,
forego the whitewashed wall.

If isolation seems radical,
omit roof
and change cube to rotunda.

This is the blueprint, my heart,
field notes to consider daily
before the butter is spread
and after the bread is eaten.

Sweet Art of Idleness

We sit, two frumps
on a log,
waiting for whales to breach.

Will they plummet,
will they spin,
course toward the shore with a pilgrim's resolve?

When two frumps sit,
it's about pursuit
deeper than whim or force of blue.

Said the emperor to the warrior
in a convolution of cherry trees,
Even if you spend your whole life
just searching for the perfect blossom,
it will be a life worth living.

A whale spouts,
two flukes per show.
Two frumps move on
in search of the perfect beachplum
upon the perfect dune.

At midday, under a perfect sky,
there are still a few stressors
but almost no intrusions of the worrisome sort.
That is why cloud-watching pays off.

Mythologies

Anywhere
is the center of the world.

In the beginning
all was under water until
we took up our positions
upon the place of emergence,
the seeded earth,
making different noises for the same reason,
nourished on cloud pollen
and flower dew.
Arctic birds winged ahead and came back.
Their feathers began to sing.

The fulmar flew over ice floes
with a flattering song
just as the people with much to carry in their sleds,
bows strung and thrummed,
were about to set out on a hunting journey
for sea mammals and reindeer.

However, they had no luck in their hunting
because Universe was sleeping,
not looking after his children.

Universe and his wife Rain Woman
had been busy billing the Northern Lights
as the flashings of spirits in combat.
The sky was so heavy in the morning,
it stole light from heaven so birds could find their way.
Universe and his wife remained in bed.

This posed a delicate problem,
yet I understood more than I saw.

I called to my steersman,
who rose and pulled up the anchor
awash in the sea,
believing only in my own mind.

From the Tower

Zealous
to the point of commitment
about the lifesaving properties
of solitude
and hating the prying of the perplexed
into one's affairs,
every solitaire
can recognize another.

Please do not enquire
nor invite us to the roundtable.
We have our own finicky forum.

This is not solipsism,
but freedom to expand.
It is not wreckage, but admiration
for its parts.

Distractions are merely
points at which thought revives,
silver over chrome,

each solitaire polishing
an overtone.

Auguries, Late August

Always on the lookout
from the observation tower
for a calamity occurring in the firmament—
a wayward fragment which, dropping
to the ground, might burn and smoke
as happened on an August afternoon,
a crashing and smoking underfoot,
wisps disappearing soon,
unassuming as a freckle
on the shoulder after sunburn.

This tendency to reveal the obscure
gives rise to many hours of conjecture
as to the sensuous aspects of a cloud,
or depth of a cave, or graves
of a walled city
and only indicates how tenuous
are the tender, soft components of some other world
with its fragrance of violets.

Preparation

Bird in the garden seeks.

Worm of a screw embeds in its wood.

Hand arranges violets in a cup.

Rubble of a room
holds certificates of honor
as issued.
(All that leverage for one crowing Chanticleer.)

Say one wants to get to the bottom
of the gloom,

to fathom it,
not sink deeper;

to design a fail-safe
for tricky maneuvers.

Final parameters not yet set
even as cold mountain air
encapsulates in channels of the down jacket
after evening vespers.

I have this to say about the headstone:
in my absence, don't change a word
or pulverize the rhythm,

and leave the lingering refrain to me.

Circumstantial Evidence

A paper curlicue
remains
of my contractual obligation to the moment.

What was there to fear when signing,
for the witnesses were the scope of day
and the hope at night of relief
from thunder.

All in all, the contract unveiled
few false positives
beyond those lodged early in my second
to third decade,
when living my life like I knew Everything
was the hapless propellant.

Let's just say there is no wreckage
up to now.
There is only instant repair.

Be it resolved
that as a member of the universe
in good standing
whose atoms will here linger in perpetual residence,
I will henceforth investigate each healing poultice.

Therefore—
welcome, once withering flowers
for (after bitterness)
it's time again to flourish.

The river has begun to flow in tempo
and (trickery of the eye)

through the green membrane
trees are leafing.
Now is felt the cosmic against the body,
known as euphoria.

Ocean Reporter

To dawdle is to find
a kind of ease:
no nitroglycerine,
just a hard look at the mists
from here.

It is Saturday
and there will be shouting
children and crowds to bear,
chatter and shining fruit at market.

Shall we?
Leave now?

One more day before rising,
before you will say,

Do you like this terrarium
which has been prepared for you?

filled as necessary—equal parts sun and water.

Lead with the left leg when rising
with the tide.
Launch like a trawler hefting its net.

Atlantic Salvor

> *Well, scholar, you must endure worse luck sometime,*
> *or you will never make a good angler.*
> — *Walton,* **The Compleat Angler**

A fine way to hold back woes
is to become, if not the compleat angler,
the compleat semi-screwed-up human engine,
ripe for analysis,
who with luck, with luck I say,
daily gets a little closer.

Just-in-time inventory:
four yellow rescue boats abreast
float when day is mellow
and in the shallows
scout blennies and butterfish
finding the storehouse empty.

It is time to give evidence—
Sky, the enforcer;
Sand, the equalizer;
Mind, the henchman.

This is not about dying
but approaching,
not about scrubbing the hull
but letting weeds muster
because destruction grieves
the common sphere.

Buff to a Shine a Perfect Day

The day came at last,
a raw, percussive magnificence,
an Easter of sorts, a dazzling
mountain of threes,
trinities, centrifugal thrusts
on three continents.

In these threes flourish escapades
the likes of which the picaresque
narratives never dream.
Three days more, three years more
to move the jelly of the previous three.

The day came at last, thrice exceeding hope
that a purple cloth cloaking mystery
will not again be seen or draped
until the third week of the following March.

Three notes from a woodwind
announce retrieval of things lost
before this day,
before the glorious tincture of this day began.

Acknowledgments

Grateful acknowledgment is made to the editors of following magazines in which these poems first appeared:

Blueline: "Momentum"
Cyclamens and Swords: "Mapping the Home Territory," "Light Lesson," "Mythologies," "At Pachelbel Farm," "A Clean Slate"
J Journal: New Writing on Justice: "Animals," "Manners at the Round Table"
The Mochila Review: "Attitude," "The Tribe that Hid from Man," "Tempus Athol Fugard," "Love Ever, Sam"
Poetry Storehouse: "Circumstantial Evidence," "Three-Season Conversation," "Dream Gazette," "Classical Music for Your Monday," "All Rise"
Rabbit Poetry Journal: "Pes Anserine"
Right Hand Pointing: "Holdings of Value"
The Seventh Quarry Swansea Poetry Journal: "Protection," "Swizzle Stick," "Striking a Chord Across Time"
Up the River Journal: "Hurricane S"
Voices Israel: "A Right Mind"
Waterways: Poetry in the Mainstream: "A Vague Unease," "Deep Attachment," "Pink and Blue"
Written River: "Life as an Enchanted State"

Original cover image, "Trojan Asteroid Shares Orbit with Earth," (PIA14404), courtesy of NASA/JPL _Caltech; author photo by Helen Mitchell; cover and interior book design by Diane Kistner; Adobe Garamond Pro text with Dimitrina titling

About FutureCycle Press

FutureCycle Press is dedicated to publishing lasting English-language poetry books, chapbooks, and anthologies in both print-on-demand and ebook formats. Founded in 2007 by long-time independent editor/publishers and partners Diane Kistner and Robert S. King, the press incorporated as a nonprofit in 2012. A number of our editors are distinguished poets and writers in their own right, and we have been actively involved in the small press movement going back to the early seventies.

The FutureCycle Poetry Book Prize and honorarium is awarded annually for the best full-length volume of poetry we publish in a calendar year. Introduced in 2013, our Good Works projects are anthologies devoted to issues of universal significance, with all proceeds donated to a related worthy cause. Our Selected Poems series highlights contemporary poets with a substantial body of work to their credit; with this series we strive to resurrect work that has had limited distribution and is now out of print.

We are dedicated to giving all of the authors we publish the care their work deserves, making our catalog of titles the most diverse and distinguished it can be, and paying forward any earnings to fund more great books.

We've learned a few things about independent publishing over the years. We've also evolved a unique, resilient publishing model that allows us to focus mainly on vetting and preserving for posterity the most books of exceptional quality without becoming overwhelmed with bookkeeping and mailing, fundraising activities, or taxing editorial and production "bubbles." To find out more about what we are doing, come see us at www.futurecycle.org.

The FutureCycle Poetry Book Prize

All full-length volumes of poetry published by FutureCycle Press in a given calendar year are considered for the annual FutureCycle Poetry Book Prize. This allows us to consider each submission on its own merits, outside of the context of a contest. Too, the judges see the finished book, which will have benefitted from the beautiful book design and strong editorial gloss we are famous for.

The book ranked the best in judging is announced as the prize-winner in the subsequent year. There is no fixed monetary award; instead, the winning poet receives an honorarium of 20% of the total net royalties from all poetry books and chapbooks the press sold online in the year the winning book was published. The winner is also accorded the honor of being on the panel of judges for the next year's competition; all judges receive copies of all contending books to keep for their personal library.

www.ingramcontent.com/pod-product-compliance
Lightning Source LLC
Chambersburg PA
CBHW070010100426
42741CB00012B/3178